What Research Says to the Teacher

The Middle School:
A Bridge Between
Elementary and High Schools

SECOND EDITION
by Sylvester Kohut, Jr.

D0095962

nea PROFESSIONAL LIBRARY
National Education Association
Washington, D.C.

The Author

Sylvester Kohut, Jr., is Dean, College of Education, Kutztown University, Pennsylvania. A former classroom teacher and curriculum consultant, Dr. Kohut is the author or coauthor of numerous books and monographs, including *Classroom Discipline: Case Studies and Viewpoints*, published by NEA.

The manuscript was reviewed by Maria Rodman, sixth grade teacher, Madison County Public Schools, Virginia; Charles F. Patton, Principal, Unionville Middle School, Pennsylvania; Jill D. Wright, Professor of Curriculum and Instruction, University of Tennessee; and Victor L. Dupuis, Professor of Education, The Pennsylvania State University.

Copyright © 1988, 1980, 1976
National Education Association of the United States

Printing History
  First Printing: September 1976
  Second Printing: January 1980
  Third Printing: October 1986
  SECOND EDITION: May 1988

Note

The opinions expressed in this publication should not be construed as representing the policy or position of the National Education Association. Materials published by the NEA Professional Library are intended to be discussion documents for educators who are concerned with specialized interests of the profession.

Library of Congress Cataloging-in-Publication Data
Kohut, Sylvester, 1942–
  The middle school.

  (What research says to the teacher)
  Bibliography: p.
  1. Middle schools—United States.   I. National
Education Association of the United States.   II. Title.
III. Series.
LB1623.K57   1988   373.2'36   88-5291
ISBN 0-8106-1079-5

CONTENTS

AUTHOR'S PREFACE
TO THE SECOND EDITION

Many pioneering middle schools established during the 1960s are now entering a third decade of operation and programming. New middle schools are being constructed and many more junior high schools are being transformed into middle schools, in part, in anticipation of the mini-baby-boom "bubble" moving into the middle-level grades.

Early proponents of middle schools can take pride in their historic commitment to educational innovation. In an effort to reaffirm the basic tenets upon which the middle school movement was founded and now luxuriantly prospers throughout the United States, this second edition provides a comprehensive update of research data with appropriate conclusions for middle school practitioners.

A middle school is *not* a building, staffing patterns, innovative curricula, or a special time schedule—it is a philosophy of education encompassing the cognitive, affective, and psychomotor dimensions of learning behavior. According to John Naisbitt (*Megatrends*, 1982), a middle school is a place where "high touch" and "high tech" are blended into a child-centered learning environment. Yet throughout the country, there are many middle schools functioning as old-fashioned junior high schools (or miniature senior high schools) disguised as middle schools in name only!

Since the early 1980s, dozens of national reports and studies on the American school have made headlines and political mileage for aspiring politicians and educational reformers. Most of the reports have focused on senior high schools, and in recent years on colleges and universities. Middle school advocates should read them with caution. Many, like *A Nation at Risk* (1983), are efficiency-driven documents that often measure success solely in terms of student test scores and downplay student diversity. All across-the-board recommendations for improving senior high schools are not applicable to middle or junior high schools. Substantive changes in middle-level education should be tempered with a clear understanding of what over twenty years of research tells us about the "in-betweener" or the "transescent" learner and this uniquely American innovation called a *middle school*.

INTRODUCTION

The emerging middle school movement throughout the United States today is, in part, an effort to rediscover, redefine, revamp, and reintroduce the basic pedagogical principles of adolescent learning upon which the junior high school was originally established almost seventy years ago.

A middle school may be defined as the school which stands, academically, between elementary and high school, is housed separately (ideally in a building especially designed for this purpose), and offers at least three years of schooling beginning with either grade five or six. A middle school functions as a separate intermediate school that combines one or more of the elementary grades with the lower secondary grades, and there is general agreement among educational planners that the ninth grade should be omitted from all definitions of the middle school. (15)*

The establishment of a new middle school or the transformation of a junior high school to a middle school program or philosophy within a school district provides a unique opportunity for professional rededication and cooperation between elementary and secondary classroom practitioners. Unfortunately, studies indicate that this ongoing reorganization of the grades in the intermediate or middle schooling years has been attributed to such basic reasons as eliminating crowded conditions in other schools within a district, justifying the construction of a new building to the school board or voters, moving the ninth grade into the senior high school, and facilitating a desegregation plan or court order. Curricular and instructional reasons for developing a middle school program often seem to be cited as secondary criteria. (1, 19, 22, 44, 54)

*Numbers in parentheses appearing in the text refer to the Selected Research References beginning on page 26.

THE MIDDLE SCHOOL

Many variables influence a middle school. Trauschke and Mooney identify the following as extremely important organizational considerations:

1. A middle school takes full cognizance of the dynamic physical, social, and intellectual changes that are occurring in young people during the 10- to 14-year-old span, and provides a program with the major purpose of creating a facilitative climate so that the transescent can understand himself and the changes that are occurring within and around him.

2. Middle schools generally locate the ninth grade, with the awesome influence of the Carnegie unit, in senior high school settings. The rationale supporting this decision is usually that ninth graders are more like tenth, eleventh, and twelfth grade students than like seventh and eighth grade students.

3. Middle schools provide opportunities for innovation. Such innovations might include team teaching, individualized instruction, flexible scheduling, and some form of continuous progress. Flexible rearrangements of time, space, materials, and people give evidence to the value of the true middle school.

4. Middle schools de-emphasize the sophisticated activities that are commonly found in the junior high school, such as marching bands, interscholastic athletics, and sophisticated dances. The program of activities which is provided permits each child to participate and is based on the personal development of the student rather than the enhancement of the school's prestige.

5. Middle schools provide opportunities for exploratory study and enrichment activities earlier than do conventional elementary schools.

6. Middle school instructional staffs combine the usual talents developed by teachers trained and oriented in the elementary school with the ability to specialize in a given field, so often a "characteristic" of a secondary teacher. (53)

Profile of the Middle Schooler

Proponents of the middle school support the rationale that children 10 to 14 years old constitute a distinct stage of development involving similar physical, (47, 42) emotional and social (17, 49, 48, 18, 8) and mental characteristics. (6)

Eichhorn introduces the term "transescence": "Transescence is the stage of development which begins prior to the onset of puberty and extends through the early stages of adolescence." (17, p. 3) On the average, the transescent child is taller and healthier than her/his group in past generations. Although performance does fluctuate, the transescent is an eager and able learner. While often displaying somewhat emotionally erratic, inconsistent, and unpredictable behavior, the transescent is highly dependent on peer group acceptance and praise rather than adult approval.

Grade Organization

In a 1963–64 NEA survey (50), only 20 of 433 U.S. school systems reported schools organized on a 5–6–7 or 6–7–8 grade pattern. In 1967, Cuff (10) identified 599 middle schools; in his 1967-68 survey, Alexander (1) identified 1,101 middle schools classified solely on the basis of grade organization. During 1969-70, Kealy (28) identified 2,298 operational middle schools. By 1992, based on grade organization and/or stated program philosophy, there will be over 12,000 middle-level schools throughout the nation.

In 1969, 60 percent of the middle schools included grades 6–7–8, 30 percent had a 5–6–7–8 vertical organization, and the remainder reflected a wide variety of patterns. (1) Today, only 50 percent are grades 6–7–8, 37 percent are 7–8, and 13 percent are grades 5–6–7–8. (1A) The most appropriate grade organization cannot be determined from the available research. According to Creek (9) and Ducas (12), sixth graders are more like seventh graders than fifth graders because of the early onset of puberty in most sixth and seventh graders. Fifth graders, on the other hand, behave more like children than like early adolescents. In separate studies, Ducas (12) and Myers (39) concluded that ninth graders are more like tenth graders than eighth graders in terms of physical, social, emotional, and intellectual maturity. These studies would tend to support the 6-7-8 grade organization for the middle school. However, other studies counter that it makes no significant difference to the educational achievement (24), self-concept (37), or attitude toward school (52) whether fifth and/or sixth graders attend an elementary or a middle school. This is definitely an area in need of additional research.

In many districts a 6-7-8 grade organization is called a junior high and in other districts a 7-8-9 grade pattern is called a middle school. According to McGlasson, (34) because of this semantic confusion and labeling problem, the grade level organization and the actual title of a school building offer no real clues as to the real curricular program or educational philosophy. Therefore, educators must address the critical question, "What is a middle school program?"

CURRICULUM AND INSTRUCTION

In many states, aside from general standards and administrative guidelines, there is no specific or mandated middle school policy. Thereby, many new middle schools or transformed junior highs have the opportunity to become unique institutions. Regardless of the type of staffing pattern or the scope and sequence of the course offerings, the two most dominant innovative features involve some form of individualized instruction and team teaching. (1)

Individualized Instruction

An integral curricular component in the middle school is the *unipac*. Although it is called by many names, basically the unipac is an individualized learning package for student self-directed study requiring the use of a multi-media resource center or laboratory. The unipac, with many organizational formats is a teacher-constructed, subject-oriented, self-instructional unit containing an overview or introduction, general and specific learning objectives, content outline, student activities section, pre- and post-unit evaluation instruments, and additional requirements dictated by a particular discipline or the interests and abilities of the student. (14)

Many middle schools attempt to provide for individual differences to some degree by introducing minicourses in the curriculum, (13, 28) while some schools even incorporate phased elective course offerings in selected English and language arts programs. (30) The establishment of a minicourse program within the middle school is a refreshing alternative to the traditional or more conventional program. Minicourse offerings vary from three to twelve weeks in length, allowing the teacher and the student sufficient time to investigate important topics selected from the pure social sciences, English, or related arts. Dupuis (13) suggests that most minicourse programs that falter do so because of a lack of commitment in terms of in-service training and continuous provisions for ongoing evaluation. His studies reveal that minicourse programs are justified because of their relevance to the "real life" curriculum, their flexibility in programming and scheduling, their tendency to encourage the use of teacher expertise and input, and their ability to meet the individual needs of adolescent learners.

Team Teaching

Team teaching maximizes teacher talent and provides opportunities for the interdisciplinary approach. The team usually provides services which include counseling, evaluating, diagnosing, teaching, and planning. Team members usually represent subject fields such as language arts, reading, social studies, mathematics, and science. (35)

Flexible and modular scheduling within the team teaching structures permits maximum planning and implementation by all team members. (21) Tobin (51) concludes that in grades five and six teaming can be achieved by all teachers teaching all subjects who are cooperatively planning specific units as a group. While in grades seven and eight, the staff can group themselves into subject areas that cross grade lines or, as in grades five and six, group themselves by grade level and assist each other in all subjects regardless of teacher specialization. School specialists in guidance, art, music, physical education and recreation, industrial arts, vocational arts, modern foreign languages, and home economics should be included in teams or should be available to meet with all groups to assist in planning and assessment.

Some teams may be composed of all elementary certified teachers and other teams may be composed of all secondary school certified professionals. Of course, staff organization is often dependent upon district or state requirements. There is no available research indicating the most desirable staffing organization for team teaching in the middle school.

Smorgasbord of Instructional Practices

In Davis' survey middle school teachers demonstrated the use of more innovative practices when compared to junior high school teachers. In terms of student educational and personal development factors, innovative teaching and organizational practices produce more beneficial results than traditional or conventional practices. (41) No two middle school programs are identical although independent and individualized instruction and team teaching are common middle school features. Innumerable instructional and modern teaching techniques are reflected in hundreds of middle school curriculum guides and brochures including small and large group instruction, closed circuit television, self-contained classrooms, intramural programs, flexible scheduling, videotaping and audio/feedback and storage units, special tutorial programs, interdisciplinary teaching, and partial and total departmentalization. (16, 32, 27, 4)

Koslick was essentially concerned with an analysis and comparison of the instructional modes employed by social studies teachers in middle and junior high schools. His study has ramifications for all middle and junior high school educators. Also a concern in his study was the effect of teacher certification upon the instructional modes employed in the classroom, the use of certain verbal behaviors on the part of both teachers and students, and the perceptions of junior and middle school teachers toward the middle school organizational philosophy, objectives, and goals. Statistical analysis of the results of his investigation reveal the following:

1. Middle school teachers did not display a use of instructional modes in the classroom that differed from those used by junior high teachers.

2. Middle school teachers did use significantly more eliciting verbal behaviors when teaching, compared to the junior high school teachers.

3. Middle school teachers with elementary certification displayed a greater use of a variety of classroom instructional modes compared to middle school teachers with secondary certification.

4. There was no significant difference between middle school and junior high school teachers in terms of understanding the philosophical purposes, goals, and actual practices of the middle school. (32)

Based on the results of his study, Koslick (32) recommends that teachers in all organizational plans should be encouraged to employ a variety of instructional modes in the classroom with special emphasis on the cognitive levels of examination and open exploration or discussion. Furthermore, school districts planning to introduce the middle school organizational scheme should provide a complete in-service program for teachers and parents so that everyone understands the basic intent of the new program.

PROFESSIONAL STAFF

The Teacher

The uniqueness of the middle school is reflected in the duties of the classroom teacher, which may include serving as a teacher-adviser, resource person, tutor, curriculum planner, seminar director, and teacher of large and small group sessions. The potential middle school educator must adequately demonstrate competencies that reveal special understandings, skills, and attitudes necessary to work successfully with the transescent in an open student-oriented climate. (38, 39) There is definite need for expanded pre-service and in-service programming for principals, teachers, counselors, and para-professionals within the middle school community. (5, 20) While the middle school movement represents a positive option for public school adolescent education in the United States, many educators have established middle school programs with almost complete disregard for pre-service and in-service training for faculty and staff. In-service workshops, summer seminars, and graduate level courses for the middle school and junior high school practitioner are of paramount importance in maintaining effective programs. (32, 46) Teachers should have the opportunity to identify specific curricular and instructional problems during in-service educational sessions and these should be the basis of investigation and study. A brief pre-workshop or pre-course questionnaire should provide valuable input for program planning as illustrated by a continuing education questionnaire from Kutztown University (Pennsylvania) for prospective middle school institute teachers. (See Appendix A.)

The Principal

If the traditional role of the teacher has changed within the middle school, then that of the principal has changed even more. As the educational leader of the school building, the principal in many middle schools serves as a part-time team member or subject matter resource person in addition to more traditional duties involving management, finance, community and parent relations, supervising paraprofessionals and nonteaching staff, and teacher performance, evaluation, and supervision. Bobroff, Howard, and Howard have investigated the professional preparation of principals and submit the following conclusion:

"... the principal of the junior high and middle school has seldom had specific training for the position. She/he clearly sees the need for such preparation and is particularly aware of the need for studying adolescent psychology and understanding the characteristics of this age group." (3)

Slate (43) suggests that a special training program for all middle school principals include a supervised internship based on performance objectives, use of simulation techniques, and definite plans for continued in-service training.

The Guidance Counselor

Because of the ambivalent natures and varying rates of maturation among emerging adolescents, they are good subjects for counseling services. Adolescents are more in need of and more receptive to the advantages gained from personal guidance than any other age group.

Stainbrook (46) and Ryan (43) are critical of the lack of coursework in counseling and guidance in intermediate teacher training. Either in specific coursework or as part of their overall professional education, middle school teachers and teacher candidates should develop an understanding of the basic skills in counseling middle schoolers. This is of paramount importance because of the teacher-advisor role of the classroom teacher.

The counselor's duties must include close cooperation with the teaching teams since students in the middle school are now beginning to consider career choices. Therefore, middle schools have both the responsibility and the opportunity to develop career education for student investigation and exploration.

The career education program in the middle school is threefold:

1. Opportunities in the subject areas to investigate many of the major careers associated with each subject area.

2. Activities outside of organized instruction which can serve as investigative opportunities concerning careers—clubs, hobbies, sports, part-time jobs, and school projects.

3. Counseling, testing and educational planning in terms of self-concept, self-awareness and career choice. (50)

Recommendations based on Arhelger's research regarding guidance services for the adolescent are enlightening and reinforce the earlier findings of Wogaman: (55)

1. Teachers, parents, pupils, and other persons in the communities should have a greater share in planning the guidance programs of the junior high schools. Teachers should participate more extensively in planned guidance activities.

2. Counselors should be relieved of responsibility of an administrative or supervisory nature, including duties connected with attendance and discipline.

3. When the number of qualified guidance personnel has been increased and greater teacher participation in the guidance program has been assured, many schools may profitably give more emphasis to heretofore neglected sources of pupil information, such as, sociograms, autobiographies, and some types of tests.

4. Group guidance activities should be augmented and subsequently integrated with the entire curriculum. The schools should utilize community resources. (2)

Neher's survey of middle school teachers reveals the need for more counselor-teacher interaction especially in matters dealing with occupational information and methods used to teach it:

1. Since the middle school system of grade grouping is flexible and adaptable to various types of exploratory programs, a broad base of occupational information should be presented to children at this stage of educational development before they are channeled into some specific type of training program at the high school level.

2. More information should be available concerning each student's occupational interests and abilities. Many kinds of career kits, tests, and even computer aids are available to ascertain the occupational aptitudes of students. The resulting data should be recorded in the cumulative records and made available to each teacher and counselor.

3. Curriculum revisions should be continuous, so that subject matter is not static or outdated, and so that it can be enriched to fit students' needs, abilities, and interests. Occupational changes related to subject matter should be considered in current curriculum studies.

4. Occupational literature and materials should be more widely avail-

able in the library, guidance departments, and classrooms. Additional occupationally oriented programmed learning units, textbooks, career kits, games, audio visual aids, and literature could be a valuable supplement to each teacher's course content.

5. Teachers would be well advised to place more emphasis on employment facts and attitudes, requirements, skills, and wages associated with the cluster of occupations related to their subject areas.

6. Follow-up studies should be made available concerning each former student's occupational history. Repeated changes in a choice of occupations following graduation may indicate a lack of occupational information and preparation. Recent graduates should be used as resource speakers to discuss problems in employment and the importance of completing high school training.

7. An increasing number of courses and workshops in occupational information should be offered to middle school teachers. Career oriented programs should be developed with supervisors and teachers of nearly all subject areas involved in the planning.

8. There is an indication of a need for more coordination between the counselors and middle school teachers in the exchange of occupational materials and information concerning individual student's specific occupational interests and abilities. It would also be advantageous to increase the number of conferences between parents, teachers, and counselors concerning students' occupational possibilities. (40)

EVALUATION

In this age of accountability it is not advisable to invest time, money, and energy into an educational enterprise unless an ongoing assessment and evaluation is provided that is based on established objectives and clear-cut goals.

Hines provides the following list of hypotheses for longitudinal research concerning all aspects of the middle school movement:

1. Pupils in the middle school become more self-directed learners than pupils in the control (traditional) schools.

2. Pupils in the middle school will have fewer and/or less intense social and psychological problems than pupils in conventional schools.

3. Achievement of middle school pupils on standardized tests will

equal or exceed that of pupils in conventional schools.

4. Middle school pupils will achieve as well as or better on standard measures of physical fitness and health as pupils in conventional schools.

5. Pupils in the middle school will hold more favorable attitudes toward school and schooling than will pupils in conventional schools.

6. Middle school pupils will hold more adequate self-concepts than will pupils in the conventional schools.

7. Social acceptance among middle school pupils will be higher than among those in conventional schools.

8. The average daily attendance record of middle school pupils will excel that of pupils in conventional schools.

9. Measures of creativity among middle school pupils will show an increase rather than a decrease during middle school years.

10. Middle school graduates will compile better academic and social records in the ninth grade than will ninth-graders from the control schools.

11. Middle school graduates will drop out less frequently from senior high school than will pupils who follow the traditional pattern.

12. Middle school teachers will more often use practices which experts generally recommend as superior.

13. Teachers in the middle school will experience a higher degree of professional and self-satisfaction than teachers in conventional schools.

14. Teachers in the middle school will utilize greater variety of learning media than will teachers in conventional schools.

15. Teacher turnover will be less in the middle school than in conventional schools.

16. Teachers in the middle school will be more open to change.

17. Teacher absentees will be less frequent than in conventional schools.

18. Patrons of the middle school will hold more positive attitudes toward objectives and procedures of the school than patrons of conventional schools.

19. Principals of experimental and control schools will have similar operating patterns within each school system. (26)

While Hines' hypotheses are suitable for legitimate and scholarly study, Georgiady and Romano (23, 41) provide less scientific criteria but an equally important practical checklist for evaluating a middle school program:

—Is continuous progress provided for?
—Is a multi-materials approach used?
—Are class schedules flexible?
—Are appropriate social experiences provided for?
—Is there an appropriate program of physical experiences and intramural activities?
—Is team teaching used?
—Is planned gradualism provided for?
—Are exploratory and enrichment studies provided for?
—Are there adequate and appropriate guidance services?
—Is there provision for independent study?
—Is there provision for basic skill repair and extension?
—Are there activities for creative experiences?
—Is there full provision for evaluation?
—Does the program emphasize community relations?
—Are there adequate provisions for student services?
—Is there sufficient attention to auxiliary staffing?

TRANSITION FROM JUNIOR HIGH TO MIDDLE SCHOOL

With the construction of many new middle schools and given the growing enthusiasm for this movement, there is a widespread feeling among some zealous middle school advocates that the junior high school is obsolete and antiquated. This is a false and unsupported assumption. Although the physical environment is important in the middle school—and everyone enjoys air-conditioning, carpets, and soft music in the halls, some of the most successful middle school programs have been implemented in old junior high school buildings with little or no renovation.

When advance planning is possible, most school districts develop a step-by-step procedure or master plan for the construction of a new middle school building and the implementation of a middle school program within the facility. The plan adopted by the Carlisle Area School District in Carlisle, Pennsylvania, represents a model middle school planning guide. (See Appendix B.) Depending on the time and resources available, a school district contemplating the transformation of a junior high school to a middle school normally develops a modification of this type of model or planning guide.

CONCLUSION

Generalizations suggested for teachers by middle school research indicate some definite trends:

1. While the 6–7–8 grade reorganization is the most common pattern, there is no available research to support any one kind of grade organization.
2. Although there are some conflicting studies, most middle school students show improvement in achievement, self-concept, and attitude toward school when exposed to innovations associated with the middle school program or when compared to students enrolled in more traditional learning programs or junior high schools.
3. There is a definite need for more pertinent research related to all facets of the middle school program in terms of curriculum, instruction, and communication.
4. There is a definite need for expanded middle-school-oriented pre-service and in-service teacher training.
5. Middle school teachers seem to demonstrate the use of more student-oriented modes of instruction and learning strategies and actually implement more innovative techniques in the classroom, when compared to teachers in more conventional junior high schools.

The middle school represents a refreshing and viable alternative to modern educators desiring a meaningful voice in the destiny of their students' academic experiences. With improved teacher preparatory programs at both the undergraduate and graduate levels (46) and relevant pre-service and in-service teacher training, middle school teachers will be better prepared for successful teaching.

The middle school is now a reality. It has finally emerged as possibly the most exciting educational enterprise in decades, for educators and students alike.

Since 1983 dozens of national reports on the American school have made headlines. Although most of the reports highlight senior high schools, some have implications for middle-level education and must be read with caution. What might be appropriate for a senior high school curriculum may well be contrary to middle-level philosophy and practice and "what-really-works" research data.

A clearly defined and articulated mission statement with corresponding objectives is evident in successful middle-level schools. Such a statement reflecting the philosophy of the school should be the result of discussions and planning among administrators, teachers, parents, students, and support staff.

A key factor in effective middle-level schools is quality student advisement. Counselors implementing this function of the guidance program work closely with administrators and teachers to help students (advisees) plan and achieve educational and personal goals. Teacher-based guidance involves different components such as the adviser-advisee role, intramurals, career education, and various group activities. The teacher's role is not limited only to homeroom or home-base periods, for advisement is interwoven throughout the curriculum and the school day with ongoing communication with parents.

Topflight middle-level schools also showcase well-organized school-home-community networking with administrators, teachers, students, and parents involved as proud shareholders in a unique educational experience.

A brand new building designed to house a middle school with an elaborate maze of rooms, laboratories, and quantities of audiovisual equipment and supplies cannot ensure a successful middle school program. The crucial ingredient is a dedicated and committed administrative and instructional staff. But dedication without adequate preparation and understanding will not suffice.

APPENDIX A

Kutztown University
Kutztown, Pennsylvania

MIDDLE SCHOOL ACTION WORKSHOP
PRELIMINARY PLANNING QUESTIONNAIRE

Years of Professional Teaching Experience   ____
Years of Middle School Teaching Experience   ____
Total Credit of Graduate Level Course Work in the Middle School   ____

The generic statements refer to curricular and instructional concerns, educational community cooperation, communication dynamics, and psychological aspects of middle school teaching.

DIRECTIONS: *Select* and *rank in order* of your professional priority the topics which should be included in an action workshop for middle school practitioners. Rank the topics from 1 through 17. The most important topic should be ranked 1 and the least important 17.

Identification, construction, implementation, and evaluation of individualized learning materials and activities ____

Interdisciplinary planning and cooperation ____

Organization of a nongraded, continuous progress program ____

Curricular innovations in the separate subjects ____

Interaction analysis and systematic observation—improving classroom climate ____

Behavioral objectives and competency-based instruction ____

Responsibilities of the administrator, teacher, paraprofessional, student, and parent ____

Staffing patterns and organizational grouping of teachers and students ____

Writing research grants for middle school teacher-oriented programs ____

Junior high school—friend or foe ____

Trends and exemplary programs in the middle school movement ____

Community participation—a public relations task ____

Introduction to the middle school—theory and practice ____

Psychology of the transescent learner ____

Teacher as the counselor ____

Physical and emotional growth of the adolescent learner ____

Certification requirements for middle school teachers—elementary or secondary orientation ____

On the back of the form, identify other major topics and activities that, from your professional viewpoint, should be included in a middle-level summer institute. (29)

APPENDIX B

MIDDLE SCHOOL(S) (7)
General Planning Outline
Carlisle Area School District

Year	Area of Concern	Activity	Personnel	Leader(s)
1974-75	Middle School Philosophy for Carlisle (Curricular and Instructional Patterns)	Read Visit Discuss Propose Alternatives	Board Central Office Teachers (6-7-8) Architect Consultant(s) Patrons Students Elementary and Secondary Administrators	Associate JHS Principal
1975-76	Educational Specifications A. Objectives B. Instructional Organization C. Curriculum D. Facilities	Committee	Teachers (6-7-8) Central Office Architect Students Patrons Consultant(s)	Middle School Principal
	Community Information	PTA Newspaper Clubs	Board Members Staff	Communications Coordinator
1976-77	Facilities	Begin construction	Architect Contractor	Architect

Year				
1976-77 (Cont)	Curricular Guidelines	Committee	Teachers (6-7-8)	Dept. Chairperson & Coordinator
	Instructional Mode	Experimentation	Teachers (6-7-8)	Dept. Chairperson & Coordinator
	Pupil Progress Reports	Committee	Teachers, Students and Parents	Middle School Principal (full-time)
	Daily Schedule	Committee	Teachers	Middle School Principal
	Athletic Program	Committee	Teachers, Students and Parents	Coordinator of Health, Physical Education
	Guidance	Committee	Counselors and Teachers	Coordinator
	Media Center	Committee	Teachers, Librarians & Students	Library Coordinator and Media Specialist
1977-78	Total Program	Simulation	Staff of Middle Schools	Middle School Principals (2)
	Parent Orientation		Staff of Middle Schools	Middle School Principals and Communications Coordinator
1978-79	Open Middle Schools			

SELECTED RESEARCH REFERENCES

1. Alexander, William M. *A Survey of Organization Patterns of Reorganized Middle Schools*. Washington, D.C.: U.S. Department of Health, Education and Welfare. 1968.
2. Arhelger, Homer. "Guidance in the Three-Year Commissioned Junior High Schools of Indiana: A Comparative Analysis, 1952-1962." Doctoral dissertation. Indiana University. 1962
3. Bobroff, John L.; Howard, Joan G.; and Howard, Alvin W.; "The Principalship: Junior High and Middle School." *NASSP Bulletin* 54-61; April 1974.
4. Bough, Max E. *Indiana Middle School Survey*. Terre Haute, Indiana: The Curriculum Research and Development Center, Indiana State University, January 1971.
5. Bowman, Jack M. "Inservice Education Programs in the Junior High Schools of the North Central Association of Colleges and Secondary Schools." Doctoral dissertation. Indiana University, 1971.
6. Bruner, Jerome S. "Inheider and Piaget's *The Growth of Logical Thinking,* A Psychologist's Viewpoint." *British Journal of Psychology* 50: 363; 1959.
7. Carlisle Area School District. "Middle Schools—General Planning Outline." Carlisle, Pa.: Area School District, September 1974.
8. Coleman, James S. *The Adolescent Society*. New York: Cromwell-Collier Publishing Co., 1961.
9. Creek, Roy J. "Middle School Rationale: The Sixth Grade Component." Doctoral dissertation. University of Pittsburgh, 1969.
10. Cuff, William A. "Middle Schools on the March." *National Association of Secondary School Principals Bulletin* 52: 135-40; May 1968.
11. Davis, Edward L. "A Comparative Study of Middle Schools in New York State." Doctoral dissertation. University of New Mexico, 1970.
12. Ducas, Wilfred P. "A Study of the Grade Organizational Structure of the Junior High School as Measured by Social Maturity and Opposite Sex Choice." Doctoral dissertation. University of Houston, 1963.

13. Dupuis, Victor L. "Shake-Up the Curriculum: Minicourse Preparation." *National Association of Secondary School Principals Bulletin* 59: 83-87; September 1975.

14. Dupuis, Victor L., and Kohut, Sylvester, Jr., "The Nongraded High School: 'Try it, You'll Like it.' " *American Secondary Education* 20-22; March 1973.

15. Educational Research Services. American Association of School Administrators and Research Division. "Middle Schools." Circular No. 3. Washington, D.C.: *National Education Association,* May 1965.

16. _____. _____. "Middle Schools in Action." Circular No. 2. Washington, D.C.: *National Education Association,* 1969.

17. Eichhorn, Donald H. *The Middle School.* New York: Center for Applied Research in Education, Inc., 1966. p. 3.

18. Faust, M.S. "Development Maturity as a Determinant in Prestige of Adolescent Girls." *Child Development* 71: 182-83; 1960.

19. Frazier, Alexander. *The New Elementary School.* Washington, D.C.: Association for Supervision and Curriculum Development, 1968.

20. Freedle, Shirley D. "An Exploration of Teachers' Attitudes Toward Selected Activities in Organized Curriculum Improvement." Doctoral dissertation. University of Tennessee, 1971.

21. Fugate, James P. "An Analysis of the Implementation Year of a Junior High School Modular Schedule as It Relates to Teachers, Students, Parents, Achievement and Grades." *Doctoral Dissertation.* University of Idaho, 1970.

22. Gatewood, Thomas E. "A Comparative Study of the Functions, Organizational Structure, and Instructional Process of Selected Junior High Schools and Selected Middle Schools." *Doctoral dissertation.* Indiana University, 1970.

23. Georgiady, Nicholas P., and Ramano, Louis G., "Do You Have a Middle School?" *Middle School in the Making.* Washington, D.C.: Association for Supervision and Curriculum Development, 1974. pp. 26-29.

24. Glissmeyer, Carl H. "Which School for the Sixth Grader, the Elementary or the Middle School?" *California Journal of Educational Research* 20: 176-85; September 1969.

25. Hicks, B. L., and Hunka, S. *The Teacher and the Computer.* Philadelphia: W. B. Saunders Co., 1972.
26. Hines, Vynce A. "Suggested Evaluation Approaches." April 1974. *ERIC* ED 093 998.
27. Kabler, Irene B. "Mills E. Godwin Middle School, Prince William County, Individualized French Program." *ERIC* ED 071 511.
28. Kealy, Ronald D. "The Middle School Movement, 1960-70." *National Elementary Principal* 51:20-25; November 1971.
29. Kohut, Jr., Sylvester. "Curriculum, Instruction, and Communication in the Middle School." *ERIC* ED 102 100.
30. _____. "Minicourses in the High School Social Studies Curriculum." *The Social Studies* 64: 169-71; April 1973.
31. _____. "Videotaped Soapbox Operas in the English Classroom." *Indiana English Journal*; Fall 1976.
32. Koslick, William F. "An Analysis of the Effect of School Organizational Plans Upon Instructional Modes in the Classroom." Doctoral dissertation. The Pennsylvania State University, 1972.
33. Lewis, James, Jr. *Administering the Individualized Instruction Program.* West Nyack, NY: Parker Publishing Company, Inc., 1971.
34. McGlasson, Maurice. *The Middle School: Whence? What? Whither?* Bloomington, Ind.: Phi Delta Kappa Educational Foundation, 1973.
35. Michigan Association of Middle School Educators. *The Middle School, A Position Paper.* MAMSE, 1975. pp. 10-11
36. Mitzel, Harold E. "Computer Technology: Its Future Role in Basic Education." *Journal of Teacher Education* 2: 124-29; 1974
37. Mooney, Patrick F. "A Comparative Study of Achievement and Attitude of 10 to 14 Year Olds in a Middle School and in Other School Organizations." Doctoral dissertation. University of Florida, 1970.
38. Mulligan, Glenn. The Relation of Selected Teacher Characteristics and Pupil-Teacher Interaction in the Classroom." Doctoral dissertation. Indiana University, 1969.
39. Myers, Norman K. "Physical, Intellectual, Emotional and Social Maturity Levels of Eighth, Ninth, and Tenth Grade Students with Implications for School Grade Organization." Doctoral dissertation. University of Missouri, 1970.

40. Neher, Lloyd D. "A Study of the Content, Scope, and Methods Employed in Implementing Occupational Information in the Indiana Middle School." Doctoral dissertation. Indiana University, 1971.

41. Nevins, James B. "A Comparative Evaluation of the Curriculum in an Innovative and a Traditional Junior High School Based Upon Certain Characteristics of Student Educational and Personal Development." Doctoral dissertation. Texas Tech University, 1970.

42. Ramey, Glenn V. "The Sexual Development of Boys." *American Journal of Psychology* 6: 217-33; 1943.

43. Ryan, William. "A Comparative Study of Beliefs and Factors Influencing the Selection of the Junior High School as a Teaching Level." Doctoral dissertation. Indiana University, 1966.

44. Simpson, George C., and Smith, George J. *Middle School Survey of New York State*. New Paltz, N.Y.: Mid-Hudson School Study Council, 1967.

45. Slate, Virginia S. "A Program to Train the Middle School Principal." *National Association of Secondary School Principals Bulletin* 59: 75-81; November 1975.

46. Stainbrook, James. "A Current and Comparative Analysis of the Professional Preparation of Teachers in the Junior High Schools and Developing Middle Schools in Indiana." Doctoral dissertation. Indiana University, 1970.

47. Stolz, Herbert A., and Stolz, Lois M. "Adolescent Problems Related to Somatic Variations." *The Forty-Third Yearbook of the National Society for the Study of Education, Part I Adolescence,* (Edited by Nelson B. Henry.) University of Chicago Press, 1944.

48. Stone, C. P., and Barker, R. G. "The Attitudes and Interest of Premenarcheal and Postimenarcheal Girls." *Journal of Genetic Psychology* 54: 61-62; 1939.

49. Strang, Ruth. *The Adolescent Views Himself, A Psychology of Adolescence*. New York: McGraw-Hill Book Co., 1957.

50. Texas Education Agency. *A Tentative Frame for Developing Comprehensive K-12 Career Education–The World of Work*. Austin, Texas: the Agency, April 1972.

51. Tobin, Warner E. "Team Teaching in the Middle School." *The Middle School Program*. Pennsylvania Association for Supervision and Curriculum Development. 23-24; May 1973.

52. Trauschke, Edward M. "An Evaluation of a Middle School by a Comparison of the Achievement, Attitudes, and Self-Concept of Students in a Middle School with Students in Other School Organizations." Doctoral dissertation, University of Florida, 1970.
53. Trauschke, E. M., and Mooney, Patrick F. "Middle School Accountability," *Middle School in the Making*. Washington, D.C.: Association for Supervision and Curriculum Development, 1974. pp. 9-12.
54. Walker, George H., and Gatewood, Thomas E. "The Status of Middle Schools in Michigan." *Michigan Journal of Secondary Education* 13: 11-15; Summer 1972.
55. Wogaman, Maurice A. "An Analysis of Guidance Organization and Services in Selected Junior High Schools in the State of Ohio." Doctoral dissertation, Indiana University, 1955.
1A. McEwin, C. Kenneth, and Alexander, William M. *Report of Middle Level Teacher Education Programs: A Secondary Survey (1986-87)*. Boone, N.C.: Appalachian State University Media Services, 1987. pp. 1, 2.

GENERAL REFERENCES

Beane, James A., and Lipka, Richard P. *Self-Concept, Self-Esteem and the Curriculum*. Boston: Allyn and Bacon, 1984.

Beane, James A.; Toepfer, Conrad F. Jr.: and Allessi, Samuel J., Jr. *Curriculum Planning and Development*. Boston: Allyn and Bacon, 1986.

Drayer, Adam M. *Problems in Middle and High School Teaching: A Handbook for Student Teachers and Beginning Teachers*. Boston: Allyn and Bacon, 1979.

Dubelle, Stanley T., Jr. *Effective Teaching: Critical Skills*. Lancaster, Pa.: Technomic Publishing Co., 1986.

Eichhorn, Donald. *The Middle School*. New York: Center for Applied Research in Education, 1966. Reprinted with new introduction, available from National Association of Secondary School Principals, 1904 Association Drive, Reston, VA 22091.

Elie, Marie-Therese. "A Comparative Study of Middle School and Junior High School Students in Terms of Socio-Emotional Problems, Self-Concept of Ability to Learn, Creative Thinking Ability, and Physical Fitness and Health." Doctoral dissertation, Michigan State University, 1970.

Fantini, Mario D. *Regarding Excellence in Education*. Columbus, Ohio: Merrill Publishing Co., 1986.

Gatewood, Thomas E., and Dilg, Charles A. *The Middle School We Need*. Washington, D.C.: Association for Supervision and Curriculum Development, 1975. A report from the ASCD group of the emerging adolescent learner.

George, Paul, and Alexander, William. *The Exemplary Middle School*. New York: Holt, Rinehart and Winston, 1981.

George, Paul S. *The Middle School: A Look Ahead*. Columbus, Ohio: National Middle School Association, 1977.

Glatthorn, Allan A., and Spencer, Norman K. *Middle School/Junior High Principal's Handbook: A Practical Guide for Developing Better Schools*. Englewood Cliffs, N.J.: Prentice-Hall, 1986.

Gruhn, William T., and Douglas, Harl R. *The Modern Junior High School*. New York: Ronald Press Co., 1947. A standard post-World War II text.

Henson, Kenneth T. *Methods and Strategies for Teaching in Secondary and Middle Schools*. New York: Longman, 1988.

Johnston, J. Howard, and Markle, Glenn C. *What Research Says to the Middle Level Practitioner*. Columbus, Ohio: National Middle School Association, 1986.

Keefe, James H.; Clark, Donald C.; Nickerson, Neal C., Jr.; and Valentine, Jerry W. *The Middle Principalship: The Effective Middle Level Principal*. Reston, Va.: National Association of Secondary School Principals, 1983.

Klingele, William E. *Teaching in Middle Schools*. Boston: Allyn and Bacon, 1979.

Koos, Leonard V. *The Junior High School*. Boston: Ginn and Co., 1972. A fine review of the early junior high school for historical perspective.

Lounsbury, John H. *Middle School Education: As I See It*. Columbus, Ohio: National Middle School Association, 1984.

Lounsbury, John H., and Vars, Gordon E. *A Curriculum for the Middle School Years*. New York: Harper and Row, 1978.

Malinka, Robert M. *Good Schools for Middle Grade Youngsters: Characteristics, Practices, and Recommendations*. Columbus, Ohio: National Middle School Association, 1978.

McEwin, C. Kenneth, and Alexander, William M. *Report of Middle Level Teacher Education Programs: A Second Survey (1986–87)*. Boone, N.C.: Appalachian State University Media Services, 1987.

Middle Grades Network. Newsletters of the National Resource Center for Middle Grades Education, College of Education, University of South Florida, Tampa, FL 33620.

Middle School Journal. Official quarterly journal of the National Middle School Association, P.O. Box 14882, Columbus, OH 43214. Excellent books, monographs, and up-to-date references that are both theoretical and practical for the middle level educator.

Myers, John W. *Involving Parents in Middle Level Education*. Columbus, Ohio: National Middle School Association, 1985.

Pringle, Ralph W. *The Junior High School*. New York: McGraw-Hill Book Co., 1937. A psychological view of junior high teaching during the pre-World War II period.

Sale, Larry L. *Introduction to Middle School Teaching*. Columbus, Ohio: Charles E. Merrill Publishing Co., 1979.

Schools in the Middle. Newsletter of the Middle Level Council of the National Association of Secondary School Principals, 1904 Association Drive, Reston, VA 22091.

Stradley, William E., and Aspinall, Richard D. *Discipline in the Junior High/Middle School: A Handbook for Teachers, Counselors, and Administrators*. New York: Center for Applied Research in Education, 1975.

Swain, John, and Needham, Richard. *In Search of Excellence: The National Reports—Implications for Middle Schools*. Columbus, Ohio: National Middle School Association, 1984.

Transescence: The Journal of Emerging Adolescent Education. Conrad F. Toepfer, Jr., ed. Two issues published annually by Educational Leadership Institute, Inc., P.O. Box 863, Springfield, MA 01101.

MIDDLE SCHOOL MATERIALS AVAILABLE FROM NEA

Order from NEA Professional Library
    P.O. Box 509
    West Haven, CT 06516
    or call (203) 934-2669
    (Be sure to include your name and address)

Classroom Discipline: Case Studies and Viewpoints, 2d ed., by Sylvester Kohut, Jr., and Dale G. Range.

Decision-Making Skills for Middle School Students, by Sherrel Bergmann and Gerald J. Rudman

Developing Positive Student Self-Concept, 2d ed., by David L. Silvernail

Developing Social Responsibility in the Middle School: A Unit Teaching Approach, rev. ed., by Phillip A. Heath and Thomas D. Weible

Foreign Languages in the Middle School (audiocassette), by William Jassey

Improving Middle School Instruction: A Research-Based Self-Assessment System, by Judy Reinhartz and Don M. Beach

Improving Spelling in the Middle Grades, 2d ed., by Maryann Murphy Manning and Gary L. Manning

Language Skills in the Classroom, by Pamela Cooper and Lea Stewart

Listening Processes: Attention, Understanding, Evaluation, 2d ed., by Paul G. Friedman

Motivation and Adolescents (audiocassette)

Reading Instruction in the Middle School (A Whole School Approach), by Maryann Murphy Manning and Gary L. Manning

Student-Centered Teaching for Increased Participation, by James Kelly

Student Team Learning: An Overview and Practical Guide, 2d ed., by Robert E. Slavin

Teaching in the Middle School (filmstrip)

Teaching the Gifted and Talented in the Middle School, by Jill D. Wright

Teaching Writing in the Content Areas: Middle School/Junior High, by Stephen N. Tchudi and Margie C. Huerta